History for Kids: The Maya, the Inca, and the Aztec

By Charles River Editors

Sacsayhuamán, the Inca stronghold of Cusco

About Charles River Editors

Charles River Editors was founded by Harvard and MIT alumni to provide superior editing and original writing services, with the expertise to create digital content for publishers across a vast range of subject matter. In addition to providing original digital content for third party publishers, Charles River Editors republishes civilization's greatest literary works, bringing them to a new generation via ebooks.

The Inca

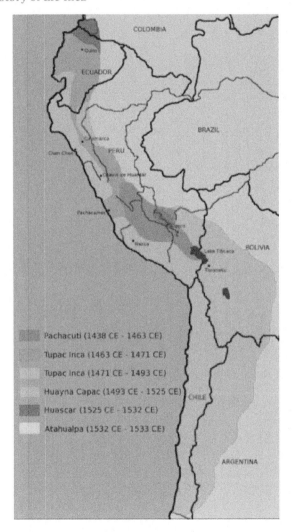

Map of the Inca Empire

The Inca always said that they were the first people to live in modern day Peru. However, there were other people there before them. It seems that the first Inca just took over their land.

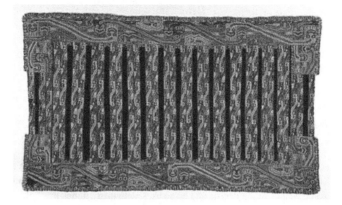

Paracas Mantle, Los Angeles County Museum of Art

Tiwanaku Vase, Tiwanaka Museum, La Paz, Bolivia Photo: Christophe Meneboeuf

The Inca believed that their people came from three caves in Cuzco, Peru. From the main cave came four brothers and four sisters. From the side caves came the people who were to be the ancestors of all the clans of the Incas.

This group then set off to find a permanent home, but among these original leaders, only one of the brothers survived. His named was Ayar Manco. The four sisters helped built the first Inca city. One of the sisters, Mama Huaca, had a son called Sinchi Roca. When the clans got back to Peru, Mama Huaca killed all the people that the Incas found there. Ayar Manco and his sisters then built houses in the valley.

At Cuzco, the Incas had good rulers and the protection of the sun god. They built a temple for him.

In 1438, the Incas were led by a man named Pachacúti Inca Yupanqui. He was a ruthless leader. Later, during the 1470s, the ruler Túpac Inca Yupanqui rebuilt the city of Quito. He also sailed out to some islands in the Pacific and came back with many things like gold and a chair made of brass.

Túpac's son made took even more land for the Inca. He later died of smallpox, brought by the Europeans to Central America. Later, his two sons, Húascar and Atahualpa, fought each other to see who would rule.

Chapter 2: Religion

Viracocha was the main Incan god. He was the creator of all things. His son, the god Inti, or the sun, was married to Mama Quilla, the moon. Inti was the father of Manco Cápac, the first Incan ruler. The Inca worshiped Inti. His High Priest was the second most important person in Peru. The god Inti was honored every year in June.

Inti, or the Sun God. Design for a flag of Peru designed by José Bernardo de Tagle, 1822

Temples to the Sun were built and kept running by religious leaders. They were given farmland called 'lands of the Sun'. Other local spiritual leaders were given food from these lands, too.

The main Incan temple was the Sun Temple in Cuzco. There was kept the great golden circle of the sun. The circle was taken by the Spanish in 1571 and sent off to the Pope in Rome. However, it never made it to Italy but was lost at sea.

Two other gold statues were put in the Coricancha by Pachacúti Inca in the 15th century. One was called Viracocha Pachayachachi. It showed the creator of everything. The other, Chuqui Ylla, showed the God of Thunder. It was to Thunder that the Incas sent their prayers for water. They built places to worship him around the Empire.

The moon goddess, Mama Quilla, was connected with the ruler's wife. She controlled the months and the calendar. Her shrines were covered in silver and run by priestesses.

Another female god was Pachamama or Mother Earth. Her special interest was farming. She too was important.

Chapter 3: Life as an Inca

The Incas spoke a language called Quechua. It may have been different from the first language they spoke before moving to Peru. They made everyone in the country speak it.

The Inca were very good at fitting into new places. They learned much about how to build their large buildings from the people that had been there before them. They also learned how to bring water down from the mountains to water their crops.

Vertical Archipelago Agriculture, Choquequirao Peru

The Incas, however, took what they learned to a new level. The rulers liked to stay clean. They built large bathtubs, with hot and cold water, in their palaces. For those less rich in Cuzco, there were public fountains beside the main streets where they could wash.

Most of Incas were farmers who worked on land given to them by the ruler of the Inca. In return for the land, the Inca farmer had to work on projects for the ruler. He also had to grow extra food for the ruler and his friends.

Inca Tunic, Dumbarton Oaks, Washington

The rulers had many outfits and changed their clothes after bathing. The males wore simple garments of rectangles of woven, died wool. These were sewn together and tied by a knot or pin. Rank was shown by headwear and style of hair. Sandals had soles of Llama leather and were held on with cords.

Inca women's clothes were a little nicer than those worn by the men. A long shift of two rectangles of cloth was tied at the waist by a belt. A second layer fell from shoulders to feet. It was closed by pins of gold and silver.

Both the male and female rulers wore jewelry, but most was worn by men. Round ear-plugs of gold or wood were worn by the men of the royal family. Other important men wore necklaces with metal disks. The most important people wore wide gold and silver bracelets. Feathers were also worn.

The Inca diet was very basic: corn, potatoes, quinoa and, sometimes, guinea pig. All the dishes were cooked by boiling or roasting them in clay ovens.

The Inca rulers also ate other small animals and even fish that were brought in from the coast by runners. Everyone drank chichi. This was made by chewing quinoa, maize or mollberries and spitting it into warm water. There it sat for a while before being drank from cups called qero.

These were made from wood or pottery.

There were men among the rulers who were story tellers. Their job was to tell the stories of the Inca's past. They did this for two reasons. First, people enjoyed hearing the stories. The story tellers did a good job making them interesting and people looked forward to hearing them.

The other reason for telling the stories was so that people would remember where they came from. The Incas did not have a way to write down what they said. People had to listen to the story tellers and learn the stories so that they could tell others later.

People would also put on plays during big parties. They sang songs and said poems they had learned about the Incan gods. Here is one of those poems:

O Creator, root of all,

Wiracocha, end of all,

Lord in shining garments (clothes)

Who infuses (gives) life

And sets all things in order,

Saying,

"Let there be man!

Let there be woman

Molder, maker,

To all things you have given life:

Watch over them,

Keep them living prosperously, (with plenty to eat)

Fortunately, (happily)

In safety and peace.

The plays may have included dances and music. This would have been played on simple instruments such as flutes, drums, panpipes and conch shell horns.

Chapter 4: The Inca Empire

The Inca referred to their own world as "four parts together." This is because the Inca divided the country into four different sections: the northwest, northeast, southwest and southeast. These four sections were connected to Cuzco by roads. Runners ran along these to deliver messages from the ruler to the governors and back again. The roads also allowed warriors to go any part of the land where they were needed. Groups of workers could move from one large building site to the next.

The roads were very important to the land. One road, the Qhapaq Ñan, ran 3,700 miles along the high Andean mountains. They connected Santiago to Quito. Other roads covered much of South America. Some people say there were more than 24,000 miles of roads. However, many of these were only small paths through the jungle.

The Incas needed their roads. There were between 4 and 37 million people in the land at any one time. The Inca ruler thought of the people of the land his family. He chose who got power and who carried out his orders.

They used the heads of the leading local families as to rule the lands they took over. These chiefs were called *curaca*. Fathers took over after sons. These people did not think of themselves as Incas. Instead, they just made sure that the Inca got their share of the money or workers owed to them. The children of these leaders were sent to Cuzco to be taught the Incan way of doing things.

Not much is known about the Inca system of law. There were most likely some local courts that made sure the people obeyed the laws passed by the Inca.

Chapter 5: Inca Buildings

An Inca Wall, Cuzco

The Inca built many of their buildings out of stone. They used stones that they cut from the mountains and out of the ground to pave roads and bridges. The Incas learned from other peoples how to paint and build beautiful buildings.

Gate of the Sun, Tiwanaku, Bolivia

Walls of The Temple Kalasasaya, Tiwanaku, Bolivia. Photo: Anakin

These buildings made up many large cities. One of these was built between two rivers. It was shaped like a puma. The Incas dug canals to bring water to the cities. They even built walls around the canals so they could not overflow and flood people's homes. 40,000 people lived in this city. Another 200,000 people lived in small villages around it.

At one end of the city - the puma's tail - was the Temple of the Sun. The walls and floors were covered with sheets of gold. The courtyard around it was full of golden statues.

Inca Masonry Photo: Hakan Svensson

Two big squares were laid out in the middle of Cuzco. One of these, Haucaypata Plaza, was surrounded with temples and great halls for larger meetings.

Typical Inca Doorway Ollantaytambo Photo Stevage

The Inca often built each new town to look like the city in Cuzco. All the roads from each of the four parts led back there. They liked to lay the city out in squares and rectangles. They did this even if they had to put roads over small hills.

Granaries or houses on hillside at Ollantaytambo

They also built their buildings in the same way as those in Cuzco. Each one was made in the shape of a square or rectangle. Each roof was made of wood and covered in dried grass.

Machu Picchu

Machu Picchu, is now the best known of Inca cities. It was a well-built city that is still around today. Some have thought that it was a fort. Others believe it to have been a work center for women. Still others say that it was a worship center or maybe hiding place for the Incas after the Spanish came. Some think that Macchu Picchu was the summer home of the Inca's rulers.

Machu Picchu Photo: Martin St.-Amant

Machu Picchu was built much like Cuzco. There were many squared off parks and places to meet. The walls of the buildings were made of stone. The rocks were cut from the ground and shaped to fit together very tightly. They stood up well, even though there is nothing holding them together.

The Inca often had to move these heavy rocks to other places far away. They did not have carts with wheels, so they moved the blocks by rolling them on top of logs.

While the Incas built very good stone walls, they did not know how to make the kind of stone roofs that the Romans and others did. So, each of their buildings only had one story. Every roof was made with wood and dried grass. The doorways and windows were made by flat stones. They could not be very wide.

Every Inca city had a great hall. People today do not really know what this used for. It may have been used for parties or big meetings. They also may have been used as houses for soldiers.

One of these great halls is still standing. It is called the Temple of the Wiraqocha. It is almost as big as a football field. Each of its long walls had 10 doorways. Fifteen of the doorways opened to the main plaza.

The So-called Temple of Wiraqocha at Puno, Peru

Chapter 6: The Spanish and the Inca

When the Spanish came to South America in the early 1500s, they were looking for gold. The Native Americans told them stories about a golden city somewhere in the Andes Mountains. A man named Francisco Pizarro wanted to find this golden city. It took him three tries, but he finally found it. The life of the Incas would never be the same.

Pizarro

In 1532 Pizarro marched into the land of the Inca. He had 168 men with him. They also had one cannon and 27 horses. As he marched along, he invited some of the Inca to go with him. Many did. They were tired of serving the Incan rulers. They wanted to do something different.

Pizarro's army first fought a battle with the natives on the island of Puná. He beat them and built a small fort there. Then his friend, Hernando de Soto, joined him there with more men. He had been further into the jungle and had met the Incan King, Atahualpa. De Soto said the king wanted to meet Pizarro.

Pizarro was excited about this meeting. He did not wait to put together a larger force of men. Instead, he marched right on into the jungle to meet the king of the Incas.

16th century depiction of Atahualpa

Atahualpa was resting in the city of Cajamarca. He had just finished a war against his brother, Huáscar. He had won the war and killed his brother. At Cajamarca, Atahualpa was getting ready to march south to Cuzco. There he would be made king.

Atahualpa still had 80,000 troops with him. However, they were tired from fighting in the long war. Many of them were also sick with smallpox.

Atahualpa was not worried about the Spanish. He had heard that they had come to his land, but he had also heard that there were not many of them. He let them come to him. He got ready for them by sending his men to camp on a hill nearby. When the Spanish got there, they found an empty city. Pizarro and his troops hid in a building off the main plaza. Then they asked Atahualpa to come meet him. The Inca ruler came back into the city. He had with him five or six thousand men, each armed with wooden clubs and spears

Pizarro sent a priest and a man who could speak the Incan language out to meet Atahualpa. The priest handed the Inca ruler a Bible. He told him that he was now to obey the Christian God. Atahualpa threw the Bible on the ground. He said he would not obey a god he had never heard of. Pizarro then attacked. His had only a few men but they were wearing armor and carrying swords and guns. They rushed out into the plaza. Then they shot the guard of nobles protecting Atahualpa and took him with them.

Atahualpa Holding the Bible from an illustration in La Conquista del Peru (Seville, 1534).

Pizarro wanted to find the treasure he had been working so hard to get. He said the Inca must pay to get their king back. He told them to bring enough gold to fill up the king's cell. They also had to bring twice as much silver.

The Incas did as Pizarro said. Then, Pizarro changed his mind. He said that he would not give Atahualpa back to them. He said that he was going to keep him prisoner. He said this was because Atahualpa had killed his own brother. Pizarro also said that Atahualpa worshipped idols and had tried to fight the Spanish. Pizarro said the king had to be baptized, then killed and his body burned. This was awful for the Inca for many reasons. One of these was that they believed that the burning of their bodies would keep them from entering the afterlife.

Portrait depicting the death of Atahualpa, the last Sapa Inca.

After killing Atahualpa, Pizarro marched south to Cuzco. There he defeated many of the Inca rulers. A priest named Bartolomé de Las Casas tried to stop him. He said that is was wrong to keep hurting people.

Las Casas later wrote a book called *Short Account of the Destruction of the Indies.* He said that Pizzaro's was like a crazy man in search of gold. He said that he killed anyone who got in his way as he marched through the area. He burned down the towns and cities to the ground. He killed and hurt most of the people who lived there.

Las Casas also talked about the stories another priest had told him about what Pizarro did. This man, named Brother Marcos, wrote about the terrible things he saw the Spanish do.

All did not go well for Pizarro. He soon argued with another Spaniard named Diego Almagro. Their argument became so bad that it finally led to a battle between each man and his followers. Pizarro won and he took Almagro prisoner and then killed him.

Before long, Pizarro's bad life caught up with him. He did not live long enough to enjoy the huge amount of gold and silver that he got. He was killed in Lima in 1541 by Almagro's son.

The end of the Inca world came quickly. The Spanish made Atahualpa's brother Manco Inca

Yupanqui the king. However, they told him that he must do everything they said. However, this did not work out like they had hoped.

Manco soon put together a group of warriors and re-took Cuzco in 1536. Still, he could not hold the city against the Spanish. He soon had to go and hide in the mountains.

The Spanish would sometimes march deeper into the jungle to fight the Incas still living there. In 1572, they took the last Incan city and killed Túpac Amaru. They believed at that time that he was the last Incan king.

The Spanish also stopped the Incan holiday, Inti Raymi. The cities of the Incan world were destroyed. The farming the Inca did was wrecked. The Spanish sent the Andeans to work in the gold and silver mines. There they were worked to death. War and hard work killed many of the Incas. European diseases like smallpox, typhus, flu, and measles killed the rest.

Depiction of Túpac Amaru, the last Inca king

Chapter 7: The Inca Today

Many parts of the Inca culture made it past the Spanish. The revolt of Manco Inca just after the Spanish took Cuzco was not the last Incan battle. In the 1700s, a man named John Santos Atahualpa said that he was the great-grandson of the Inca ruler killed by the Spanish. He put together a large force of warriors to fight the Spanish in the jungles of Peru. He made his own country and made the Spanish priests leave. However, the Spanish soon got control back over the country.

Another war was led by Túpac Amaru II in the 1700s. The Spanish army had a hard time beating him. Túpac was taken with his family to Cuzco in 1780. There he had to watch while his wife and children were killed. Then he was taken to the main plaza and killed.

Túpac's followers left the two cities they had begun to build in the Vilcabamba Valley. They went to hide in the jungle. There are tales that somewhere in the jungle of Peru, the last of the Incas built a city called Paititi. They also say that they hid a great store of gold there.

To this day some people still search for the lost last Inca city and its store of gold. After Túpac's war, the Spanish said that people could no longer speak Quechua. This was just another way for them to destroy a culture that was proving far too hard for them to kill.

Túpac Amaru II

From the beginnings of Spanish living in the area up until the present day, the Incas have lived in one form or another. The Spanish were never able to wipe them out.

In 1632, a man named Juan Sicos Inca wrote a story about a parade he watched go through the streets of Cuzco. At the front of the parade march a Catholic priest carrying the banner with the picture of the Virgin Mary on it. Juan marched in the parade himself. He wore chains of pearls, gems and gold like his people had for years. However, he also wore Spanish armor, a sword and a dagger.

Following the banner of the Virgin in the parade was a second one held by three natives. They were dressed in the "ancient style". The icon they were carrying, a canvas painted on both sides, was all Inca. This combination of Christian and Inca religion still goes on to this day.

The Inca culture did not just survive in Peru. It also became an important part of the lives of Europeans. They were very interested in stories of the Incas. They really liked stories of the Inca rulers.

One man from Poland went to Peru and fell in love with an Inca princess. The two married and had a daughter named Umina. She later married the nephew of Túpac Amaru II. This nephew got all the old stories from his uncle. The story goes that these old stories were written down and taken to Poland. However, they were lost and never seen again.

In France, an Inca princess was given life by the popular writer Françoise de Graffigny. She wrote a book in 1747 called Letters of a Peruvian girl. In the story, the Inca princess Zilia, is writing to her fiancé the Inca Aza. She tells him of her kidnapping from the Temple of the Sun by the Spanish. She then says that she was rescued by French sailors and went to live in France.

Then there is the play, *Alzire*, written by the famous Frenchman Voltaire. It was first put on in Paris in 1736. It is the love story of the Inca princess Alzire. About 100 years later, a man named Verdi later wrote an opera, *Alzira*, based on the play.

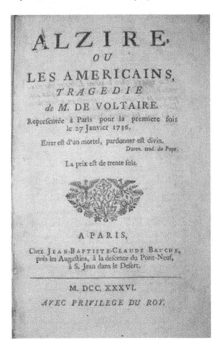

In Peru, the Inca have had a long life that is more real than that shown in European plays. Peru left Spain in 1821. However, this did not do much to help the native people. In fact, it hurt many of the Andean natives. The strict laws on the control of the land made the problems that are still going on today. Most of the modern Inca still work hard to hold on to their culture in a way of life that is strange to them.

In the 1920's, a plan began in Peru to bring back the Incan style of government. They also began to celebrate Inti Raymi again in 1944. Each leader in a town dressed as an Inca king. He then marched in a parade in front of native Andeans and tourists. The "Inca ruler" then speaks to the crowd in type of Incan language that more than 2 million people still speak. The festival involves a many actors and dancers. It follows a script that was made up from the writings of Garcilaso de la Vega.

Pictures of Inti Raymi Festival (Festival of the Sun) at Sacsayhuaman, Cuzco. Photos by Cynthia Motta

Chapter 1: The Mystery of the Maya

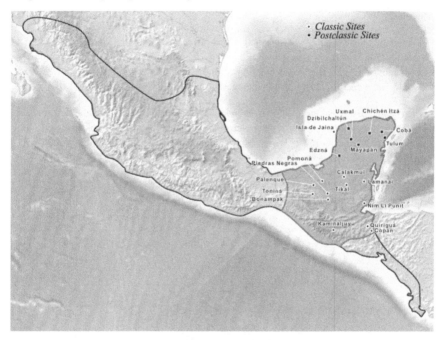

Map of the Mayan Empire

Most people know very little about the Mayans. Even people who have studied them for years still don't understand much about them. They still have questions. One question is, "Where did they come from?" Another is, "What caused them to go away?"

Why don't people know the answers to these questions? The main reason is that when men came from Europe to America, they tore down a lot of Mayan cities and buildings. There were no big battles because most of the Mayans were already gone.

Catholics from Spain came to South America. They brought along priests who wanted to turn the Mayans into Christians. They taught the Mayans that their religion was wrong. They wanted them to become Catholics. When the Mayans did, they gave up their other religion. This means very few people know much about the Mayans' old religion.

Although the Spanish killed many Mayans, they also wrote down a lot about them. A Catholic priest, Bishop Diego de Landa, wrote a book about the Maya in 1566. He drew pictures of what they looked like and the clothes they wore. He also copied down the letters of their alphabet and their words. But he and his men also burned many of the books the Mayans had written about themselves.

Many of the Mayans' buildings were also broken apart. Sometimes the Spanish used the stones they took from old Mayan houses and temples to make new buildings. However, the Spanish didn't find all of the Mayan buildings. A lot of them were deep in the jungle where no one could find them. People are still finding new Mayan buildings today.

When people first found these old Mayan buildings 200 years ago, they thought they might have been built by the Greeks or Romans. Then a man named John Lloyd Stephens wrote a book about the Mayans in 1843. Many people read the book and came from all over the world to learn more about the Mayans.

Many of these people wondered what the buildings they found had been used for. They tried to guess but often got it wrong. For instance, they called one building a castle. This could not be true because of the way it is built.

These two buildings are called the Pyramid of the Magician and the Building of the Iguana. They are in the Mayan city of Uxmal. These names came from Europeans or Americans. They're definitely not what the Mayans called the buildings.

This building is called the Castle at Chichén Itzá. It's a great building, but it probably wasn't a real castle.

Chapter 2: The Start of the Maya Civilization

Most people think the Aztecs were the biggest group of people in South America. This is not true. The Mayans were just as big as the Aztecs. They lived in much of South America.

The first Mayans hunted animals for meat. They also gathered berries and vegetables that grew in the jungle. They may have first come from Asia more than 15,000 years ago!

Later, the Mayans became farmers. They stayed in once place and grew food to eat. They grew corn, beans and squashes. When things would not grow well on the land they had, they would use new land. They did this by cutting the trees down and burning them. This made the soil better for gardening.

About 4,000 years ago, the first Mayans were called Olmecs. They built cities near their farms. We don't know much about them, but we do know two things. First, they built pyramids that looked a lot like the ones in Egypt. Second, they played a ball game that is a lot like the game of lacrosse.

A pyramid at the city of El Mirador

Buildings at the city of Tikal

Chapter 3: Life in a Maya City

The most important person in any Mayan city was the king. He had helpers who were the best warriors in his city. The Maya believed that the king had to do certain things to keep them safe and happy. They wanted him to be able to do these things, so they took good care of him. They brought him plenty of food. They also helped take care of his house and land. They even built new buildings for him.

This Mayan art shows King T'ah 'Ak' Cha'an

Besides the people that lived in his own city, the king also controlled some of the people who lived near him. He made them give him things like jewels, cotton, honey and salt.

When a Mayan king had to do something special, he dressed up in fancy clothes. He had different clothes for different times. He also wore a huge crown made of wood. It was painted and covered in feathers, shells, jewels and fabric. Sometimes a crown would have a picture of one of the Mayan gods on it.

Mayans thought that having a big nose was a good thing. They would put putty on their noses to make them look bigger. They would also tie a board around a baby's head to make its nose take a special shape. Kings and important people wore fancy earrings. They even made holes in their teeth and filled the spaces in with jewels.

One king that we know more about was King Pakal. Several years before he died, he had a tall pyramid built into a hill. It had five different doors and stairs running to the top. It also featured a list of all his family members. One stairway leads down into the middle of the pyramid. When he died, his body was put there. He was wearing many necklaces and a face mask made of jewels and shells. His body was in a painted coffin. On the lid of the coffin was a carving of King Pakal. It showed him going down into the underworld.

A statue of King Pakal's head

This carving was on King Pakal's tomb

When this place was found in 1951, it also had five skeletons. They were four males and one female. These people had been killed so they could help Pakal in the underworld!

Everyone in a Mayan town had a certain place. The king was the most important person. Then came the nobles. A man was a noble if his father had been one. If both his father and mother came from noble families, he was even more important.

Some of the nobles were rich farmers. Others were rich store owners, priests and warriors. They had to keep stories about the history of the city. They could do this by making sculptures or writing things down. The nobles also made the calendar and tried to predict the future. They even fought in wars and made money for the city.

The next most important people were the free workers. They each had a small bit of land to work on. They shared what they grew with the king and temple priests. The Mayans believed that neither good things nor bad things happened by luck. That is why they studied the patterns of the sun and stars. They believed these patterns were put there by the gods to help the Mayans know what would happen.

The Mayans had laws and punished those who broke them. A man might have his head crushed if he did something very bad. If he stole something, he might have to be someone's slave for a while. That was bad because a slave was the worst thing to be in a Mayan city. Most of them had been taken away from their homes during a war. A lot of them were killed by the Mayans. The Mayans thought killing slaves would make the gods like them more.

Most of the people living in Maya cities were farmers. They lived in huts made out of wood. These huts were built up on platforms. The farmers were important because they grew the food everyone ate.

Depending on where he lived, a Mayan farmer might have a harder or easier life. If he lived in the north, he would have to work hard to grow food. He would often have to clear new land when the old land would not grow anything anymore. In other places, there was lots of water. This made it easy to grow vegetables to eat.

Farmers who lived near the ocean often grew things in land that was very wet. They would have to build up dirt into mounds to plant their crops on.

Mayan farms grew many different crops. They mostly grew mainly corn, beans and squashes. In some Maya towns, they grew cotton, cocoa and honey too. If they didn't eat everything, they traded the food with other towns near them.

The Mayans often ate animals that they hunted. Along the ocean, the Maya had a diet that included lots of fish.

When a Mayan town would run out of space for its farms, it would try to take land belonging to another town. This would lead to a war. This happened a lot because there was not enough rain to water the crops. It could also happen if there were too many people living on the land.

We don't know much about how the Mayans fought. Most of their cities did not have walls around them. This meant that their men would go out to meet the enemy away from where the women and children lived. Some of the groups of Mayans fought more often than others. It is likely that when they did fight, it was very bad. If they took someone prisoner, they would most likely kill him right away. If not, he would be a slave. That meant he was probably killed later for the gods.

Chapter 4: The Myths and Religion of the Maya

Like most people, the Mayans told a story about how the world began. This story starts out with the big flat earth stuck between 13 levels of heaven above it and nine layers of underworld below it. At the four corners of the world, trees hold up the heaven. At the center of the world is a big tree that held everything together.

Before there was a world, there was only sky and water. In the water lived a god called Gucumatz. His named meant Sovereign Plumed Serpent. In the heavens lived the god Huracán. His name meant Heart of the Sky. The sky god and the sea god met and talked. This talk made the world come alive.

Gucumatz and Huracán talked about the earth. This caused the waters to move apart. The earth rose up, mountains came out, and forests, lakes and streams came together. The two gods also talked about who should live on the earth. This is how animals were created.

A Mayan sculpture of the god Gucumatz

Like many gods, Gucumatz and Huracan could change the way they looked. Huracán was a one-legged god. The god Gucumatz was sometimes like a snake with feathers. Gucamatz and Huracán belonged to groups of sky and sea gods.

The animals could not speak. They were not able to honor the gods like Gucumatz and Huracán wanted them to. The gods talked and agreed to make people. At first, they tried to make men from mud. But when it rained, the men fell apart. Then they tried to make men out of wood. But the wooden people they made had empty hearts.

The gods made a flood to get rid of the wooden people. The animals and the stone corn grinders rose up and killed all but a few of the wooden men. A few lived, so the gods let them be monkeys. But they were still not able to praise the gods.

The gods next tried making a man from corn. This was the most important food for the Mayans. The gods took corn to a grandmother goddess, Xmucané. She made maize paste. The gods tried to make human flesh out of it. They squeezed out some of the water and used it to make blood. They made four men. These men became the fathers of the four K'iche clans. These humans could work and give thanks to the gods.

The men they made also had good hearing and could see very well. But their ears and eyes were so good that they could see and hear too much. The gods did not like this. They decided to make the men see and hear less well. These men were soon joined by women.

Chapter 5: Math and Writing

0	1	2	3	4

5	6	7	8	9

10	11	12	13	14

15	16	17	18	19

This shows how the Mayans wrote their numbers

Our math is based on units of 10, like our fingers. Maya math is based on units of 20, like their fingers and toes. To show the numbers 1 to 4, they used dots. Five was written with a line, and 6 was a line with a dot above. Up to 19, the Maya were able to use a dots and lines. The zero was written as a shell. Written numbers helped them count things they traded. It also let them record time and make a calendar.

The Maya used many calendars. One had 12 months that were 20 days long. It was used for praising the gods. But they also used a 365 day calendar. It had 18 months that had 20 days each. There were also five extra days at the end of the year.

The Mayan also had a Long Count calendar. This calendar started with the beginning of time. It goes back to August 11, 3114 B.C.! Time was measured from this starting date. Using this Long Count calendar, the Maya gave the dates of important events, like when a man became king. A lot of people thought the Long Count calendar said the world would end in December of 2012! These people didn't understand the Mayan calendar though.

Time was very important to the Mayans. The past, the present, and the future were all important. The Mayans planned social activities on their calendars.

On most days, the Maya used the 12 month calendar with 20 days each. Each month had a name. Men would use this calendar to decide the best time for different activities. A priest kept track of what day it was.

The planet Venus was very important to the Maya. They even built a special place to stand and look at Venus in one city. They built it at a place known as Caracol. It has three doors to the inner chamber. They line up with positions in the sky where Venus can be seen.

Caracol

The Mayans had a great system of writing. For a long time, modern people did not know what it meant. Then they learned that the Mayan used both pictures and letters to spell out a name. For example, the Mayan word for jaguar could be shown by drawing the head of a jaguar or it could be spelled with letters. The Mayan language was read from left to right, just like the English language.

In most Maya cities, there was at least one ball court. The ball game was called pok-ta-pok. It was very important. The courts were big rectangles with walls on each side. Each team had 2-7 people. They would hit a rubber ball with their bodies, but they couldn't use their hands or feet.

A Mayan Ball Court

The best way to move the ball was by using the hips. The teams tried to make the ball go through a round ring attached to the long wall of the court.

The Mayans thought the ball game was the most important part of their lives. Games were so important that the losers were sometimes killed for the gods. Some people think the Mayans used ball games to settle arguments and fights.

Chapter 6: Cities

The first great Maya city was built about 2,200 years ago. It was in El Mirador, Guatemala. Thousands of people lived there. At one end of the city was a huge pyramid. It's the tallest Maya pyramid still around. It was about as tall as a 20 story building! There are two temples beside it

On the lower levels of these temples, people have found jaguar masks. Next to these temples was a burial place. It held the bodies of priests and noblemen. There were also beautiful black rocks called obsidian. There were also stingray spines. These were used by the priests as part of their worship of the gods. The priests would use them to cut different parts of their bodies. While they did this, they would call out to the gods to hear them. On the other end of the city was a smaller pyramid. It also had a temple on each side of it.

The city of Tikal was a small village. People first lived there about 2,900 years ago. 400 years after they moved there, they built a small temple on the highest point of the city. From the top of that temple, they were able to look up into the night sky. They could see Venus and the moon and many stars.

The Temple at Tikal

About 2,000 years ago, they built the Great Plaza of Tikal. This was a huge place. It took them more than 200 years to finish it. When they finished one building, they would start another one.

About 1,500 years ago, Tikal became one of the most powerful cities in the area. They had many great and powerful kings. The kings worked hard to make sure the city was safe. They would fight wars to keep their city strong and happy. They also made deals with other Mayan cities. Each city would agree to help the other one out.

One of the most famous kings was Hasaw Chan K'awil. He fought the Calakmul people in

696. They had once attacked Tikal and destroyed a lot of it. But when Hasaw Chan K'awil was king, he made sure they would never hurt his people again. His son, Yik'in Chan K'awil, began building more new places in Tikal. During his life, he built five of Tikal's most important temples. He buried his father's body in one of them. Around the year 900, Tikal finally fell down. The people left it and went to live somewhere else.

Most of the cities built by the Mayans were finished around 1,200 years ago. The best Mayan buildings were there. One of those cities was called Uxmal. At Uxmal, a king named Lord Chak built several of the largest buildings. These included one that was called the Nunnery. Of course, the Mayans didn't actually use it as a nunnery.

These same men called another building the Governor's Palace. The decorations on these buildings included fancy carvings. These were made on flat and rounded stones. They used different patterns in their building stones too. This made the building one of the best places still standing.

People think these cities liked each other. That's because they had roads that ran between two cites called Kabah and Uxmal. It was decorated with a large arch. Arches were very hard for people to build. It shows people today how smart the Mayans were.

Arch over the road from Kabah to Uxmal (Photo: Alan McNairn)

Today, people love to visit places where the Mayans once lived. The Mayan city that most people visit is called Chichén Itzá. It was once very large and became a very important city. It has a huge pyramid with lots of decorations. There is also a huge ball court. There is a tall place to look at the stars. There are also many temples.

The builders of this city made buildings that were even better than those at Uxmal. They built tall, round columns and put fancy decorations on the outside of their buildings.

Many people who go to visit Chichén Itzá want to see the sacred cenote. The cenote was a large hole in the ground that was full of fresh water. You can only get to it by a road from the plaza. It was a place for the Mayans to give thanks for water. It also gave the people plenty of water. They had to have water to make their crops grow. The Maya thought the cenote was very important.

The people of Chichén Itzá made offerings to the Mayan rain god Chaac. They threw things into the cenote to give thanks to Chaac. Sometimes, they even threw people into it! Chichén Itzá was a great city, but people only lived there for about 150 years.

A temple at Chichén Itzá

El Castillo at Chichén Itzá

The last big city the Mayans made was Mayapán. It was built around 1200 A.D. and lasted until right before the Spanish came. Its buildings were not as good as those in other Mayan cities though.

Chapter 7: The End of the Mayans?

The Mayans had a lot of great cities. But they began to have fewer and fewer people. Cities in the southern part of the Mayan lands started to die out. The ones in the north were empty 100 years later.

No one knows why the Mayans left. Most of their people were gone by the time the Spanish got to South America in the 1500s. Only a few Mayan families stayed. Some people still live in the jungles today. They claim that the Mayans were their ancestors.

One part of the Mayan culture is still alive today. About 6 million people speak one of the Mayan languages. Others still have religious beliefs that are like those of the ancient Mayans. There are also many books that have stories from the Mayans themselves. The world is still interested in them. This means the memories of the Mayans will live on into the future.

The Aztec

Chapter 1: The History of the Aztecs

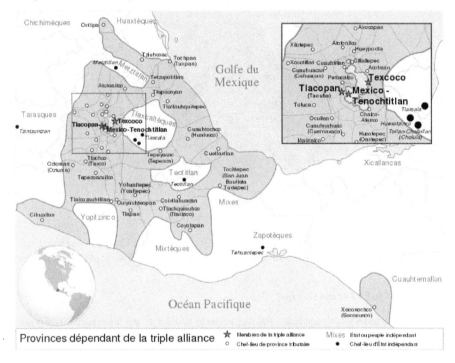

Map of the Aztec Empire

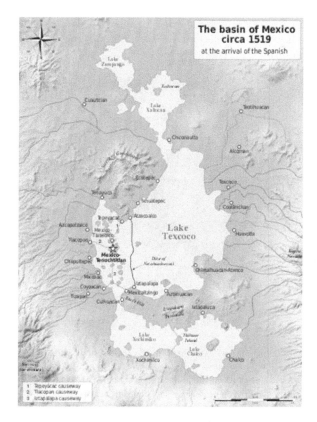

The area in Mexico where Aztec cities were.

The Aztecs arrived in the valley of Mexico in about 1250 A.D. They came from a city named Aztlan to the north. Aztlan was on a beautiful island in a lake. It is likely that the Aztec people came from somewhere in the modern state of Nayarit in Mexico. This is on Mexico's west coast, near the Pacific Ocean.

There were other people in the Valley of Mexico when the Aztecs arrived. They made their own culture and way of life. They did this by taking in different parts of other cultures and religions in Mexico. When the Aztecs built their major cities, they were like those built by other people around 100 B.C.–250 A.D. The Aztecs made a god from the Toltec people their own, and made a religion around his worship.

The Aztecs actually lost one of their first important battles. They tried to settle on the shore of

Lake Texcoco but were kept away from the city. They then moved further south to Culhuacán. There, they were paid to fight for other nations. Eventually, the people of Culhuacán made the Aztecs leave their land.

A drawing of the Founding of Tenochtitlan, It's from a book called the Codex Mendoza.

In 1325, the Aztecs came upon an island in Lake Texcoco. There they saw an eagle roosting on a cactus while eating a prickly pear. They said the eagle was Huizilopochtli, their war and hunting god. They said the red fruit was a heart. The island was just like their other home in Aztlan.

For much of the 1300s, while they built their city of Tenochtitlan, the Aztecs worked for the more powerful cities around the lake. When building their great city, they divided it into four sections. Each section was divided into smaller sections. Each of these 24 sections was made up of families. Each had a temple, markets, schools and offices. Each was led by elders. These elders formed the government of the city. They even chose the king and managed the city.

From 1409-1428, the Aztecs made peace with their neighbors, Tlacopan and Texcoco. This was called the Triple Alliance. It allowed the Aztecs to get bigger without the being afraid of what the other towns might do.

In 1426, the rulers made the war lord Obsidian Serpent their kings. He chose Snake Woman to rule with him. Together they made their land stronger. They beat the cities around the lake and made them pay taxes. Over the next 100 years, the Aztecs would become more and more powerful. Their last ruler, Montezuma, became king in 1503. He ruled until the Spanish conquered the city in 1520.

Chapter 2: The Aztec Empire

Making one man the king became possible because of an agreement made by the Aztecs in 1420. The Aztec territory grew quickly under the rule of the all-powerful kings. This was the time of the Aztec Empire. When they beat a city, the Aztecs took people for slaves and charged taxes. These were sent to Tenochtitlan on a regular basis. The Aztecs did not leave soldiers behind. Instead, they just went home with their slaves. It was left up to the people left in the city to send in their taxes when they were due. Those cities that did not pay would be attacked again and more slaves taken. The Aztecs did not even have an army. They just called warriors to serve as they were needed.

The Aztecs had to grow. They had too many people to feed on the land they had. When they needed more, their warriors were sent to take new countries and charged more taxes. Of course, as time went on the new cities were located further and further away from the capital. The Aztecs found the land to the west and north was not good enough to bother with. To the south, the taxed cities gave them lovely items. However, they were too far away to send food. So it was to the east that the Aztecs began building their land. But as they went further away, less and less food could be sent. This was made worse by the fact that the Aztecs had no wheeled carts or big animals to carry the food.

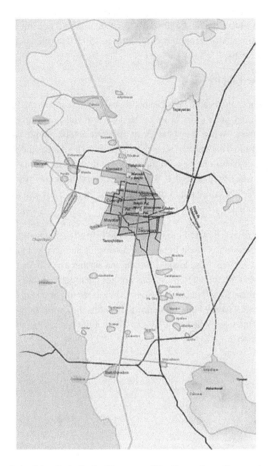

Tenochtitlan and the islands in Lake Texcoco. The lines show the routes people took to the towns around Tenochtitlan. This map was made by Hanns Penn.

As a result, the Aztecs had to rely on humans to carry in the taxes. This made a new problem. The further these humans had to carry food, the more of it they ate along the way. Thus, the cities that supplied food to the Aztecs were within easy reach of Lake Texcoco.

Another important fact was that the Aztecs' capital was on an island. This meant using water for travel. As many as 10,000 canoes, some of them as long as 50 feet, were often sailing on the lakes in the Valley of Mexico. They brought goods across Lake Texcoco from farms and villages. They also carried taxes from towns further away.

The farms in the Valley of Mexico were special. They were built on mounds of earth in the shallow waters. The natives were able to make small, floating islands by digging the mud from the lake's bottom and piling it up. Some of these islands were almost 100 feet long. These farms grew a lot of food. However, they were easily hurt by changes in the water level. These farms later covered about 25,000 acres around Lake Texcoco.

King Ahuítzotl (1486-1501) grew the empire to include the cities of Mitla and Oxaca. These were part of present day Guatemala and El Salvador. From this region, the Aztecs took taxes in the form of cotton, jade, jewels, feathers and cocoa. In 1440, the city of Taxco was beaten. It sent cotton, honey, and coral to Tenochtitlan. Far to the south, the Aztecs had traders who traded goods for the materials needed by the artists in Tenochtitlan.

The Aztec Empire was based on farming. The rulers got the taxes from the farmers and fishermen of the city. They gave out the extra as gifts to the people to keep everyone happy.

Chapter 3: The Aztec City of Tenochtitlan

Today Tenochtitlan is mostly remembered for being a floating island city. Lake Texcoco had many shallow lakes and marshes. It was on this lake that the floating city was built.

Tenochtitlan depended on water management for the safety of the city. The Aztecs made amazing things to move water to improve farming and transport things. The Aztecs controlled the water in the lakes and marshes. They made sure the water did not get too salty. By working hard, the Aztecs made sure that the god of water who controlled rain and storms, was happy. They built two worshipping areas on the great central pyramid of Tenochtitlan.

Fresh water was first supplied to the city by two channels made of reeds and mud. These ran from Chapultepec, and gave people water for use in their homes. The two channels also sent water to underground which supplied water to the palaces in the center of the city. The running water was used for baths, pools and gardens.

At one time, a huge structure to move water was built. It was over 20 feet wide and ran for 10 miles. As the city grew, an even bigger system was built in 1499. It brought water from five springs into a lake in Coyoacán.

Since they could not really keep these structures from overflowing, they could be dangerous. In 1500, there were heavy rains. There was a terrible flood. Many people lost their homes.

The Aztecs used a lot of water for bathing and washing their streets. Thousands of men watered and swept the streets daily. The rulers also kept themselves clean by using soap to bathe. The king bathed twice a day in tubs in the royal palace. He also often changed his clothes.

The Aztecs were careful in how they took care of waste. No one was allowed to put solid waste through the pipes that went into the lake. Care was taken to collect solid waste and use it on the crops.

By the time Tenochtitlan was taken by the Spanish, it spanned 10 million square meters. The size and style of Tenochtitlan was so amazing that when the Spanish arrived, many said it was like Venice in Italy. The number of people who lived there was also amazing. 60,000 people could do business in just one market. The market had a many different things for sale. There were also many artists who made and sold their goods.

This is a model of Temple Precinct at Tenochtitlan. Photo taken by Thelmadatter

The city was built around the walled square of the Great Temple. The homes of the king, priests and warriors were nearby. The streets were laid out in straight lines. Between the streets were canals that brought in water. Bridges connected the city to the mainland.

Ruins of Templo Mayor

In the middle of Tenochtitlan was a walled area. The wall was decorated on the outside with snakes, so it was called the serpent wall. Inside was a large park with a huge pyramid in the middle. This was the home of the Great Temple. It was built and rebuilt several times over the years. The last Great Temple was built in 1487. It was about 130 feet tall.

Model of the Temple

On top of the pyramid were two temples, one for each of the Aztec gods. The Aztecs' temples were built to show the movement of the sun throughout the year. In the wetter season, the sun rose behind one temple. In the summer, it rose behind the other. On the two mid-season days the sun rose between the two temples.

In the walled park, there were five other buildings. There were temples to less important gods. There was also a ball court where games were held. Many of these games had teams hitting a ball through a goal using their hips or chests or heads.

The common people of Tenochtitlan lived in houses that faced the streets. They were built of mud and brick or mud over woven sticks. Each was L-shaped and had a courtyard in the middle. This is where the family spent much of its day. The women spun thread and wove fabric, ground corn, baked tortillas, prepared food and visited with each other. Families also held parties to welcome new babies or naming a child. During these parties, everyone enjoyed lots of food and drink. The men worked on their nets or fished in the lake.

Almost 300,000 lived in the city. Most of these were working people. Many were slaves.

The city had things that were no one in Europe had ever thought of. For example, there were schools for all children, rich and poor. Next to the local temple were the schools for children from 7 to 14 years in age. Boys and girls were taught in different rooms. Children were taught the history of the Aztecs. They also learned dancing, singing and public speaking. They were even taught religion. The schools for children of the rulers were in the center of the city. There they were taught more. They learned astronomy, arithmetic, proper speaking, reading and writing.

The priests and warriors lived in fancy houses near the royal palace. These buildings were decorated with sculptures. They may have been colorfully painted outside and inside.

The king lived on the second floor of his palace with two wives. He also had many servants, guards and helpers. To feed all these people, the palace had large kitchens and store rooms. Large dinners included many dishes. These included frogs with green peppers, sage locusts and fish eggs. As many as 300 guests were fed at big parties. While the king ate with his guests, he was hidden behind a screen during the meal.

The king Montezuma I made laws about how the common dressed. Their clothes were made of cotton. They were also not allowed to wear sandals in the city streets. Some cloaks, jewels and decorations could only be worn by certain people.

Chapter 4: Aztec Art and Architecture

The Aztecs showed great skill in their art, though their pictures often showed terrible things. Their art showed good form and arrangement.

Sadly, much of their art was destroyed. The Spanish tore down the city of Tenochtitlan. The Aztecs who escaped the Spaniards' swords and the new European diseases disappeared into the jungle. Meanwhile, the buildings of the city were torn down to get stones to build a new city on the site. Until recently, there was nothing left of the once mighty Aztecs. Because of the nature of their empire, the Aztec culture did not get into the other cities that paid taxes. Still, bits and pieces have Aztec art been found around the area.

**A sculpture of the god Coatlicue. It's in the Museum of Anthropology in Mexico City
now. This photo was taken by Rosemania**

Most of the treasures that the Spaniard Hernan Cortés and his followers took from the city
were melted down or otherwise used. The first shipment of the treasure arrived in Europe in
1520. It was looked over by the German artist Albrecht Dürer. He was very impressed by a gold
sun and a silver moon that he said were nearly 6 feet across. The shipment also included strange
costumes, weapons and metals. Durer said it was very valuable. He wrote, "I have seen among
them wonderfully artistic things, and have wondered at the subtle [genius] of men in foreign
lands."

The rest of the Aztec art was destroyed by priests who quickly tried to convert the Aztecs to
Christianity. Aztec papers were burn, but a few survived. These were copied by later children
and grandchildren of the Aztecs. The sculpture that trimmed the palaces and temples were
destroyed.

Much of Aztec sculpture shows people being offered to their gods. To the Spanish, One of
Cortés' soldiers said that when he saw these gold and jewel images in a temple, they were
covered in blood.

A sculpture of "she of the serpent skirt", found in the temple precinct in the 1700s, is a truly scary image. The head is gone. In its place are two facing serpent heads. The hands and feet of the god are clawed. She has a necklace decorated with cut of hands and hearts. The god was said to live in a temple on a rise called the hill of snakes.

The sculpture show what good artists the Aztec were. Great care was taken to make the fine lines. They meet to make rounded shapes. It was once painted in bright colors and covered with jewels and gold.

The Great Calendar Stone. It's now in the Museum of Anthropology in Mexico City.
Photo: Rosemania

Also found near the Cathedral in Mexico City in the 1700s was the Great Calendar Stone. It is the most famous piece of Aztec art. People have made hundreds of models of it through the years. The skill of Aztec sculptors is clear. In the center is the face of a female god. It is framed by clawed arms that hold human hearts. This is surrounded by signs of the four suns. This shows the end of the world. The next circle has the names of the 20 days in the Aztec calendar. This stone was not part of a temple. It was laid out flat and served as a site of sacrifice to prevent the end of the world.

Pendant Mask, at the Louvre, Paris

Aztec artists made sculptures that were often different from carvings that were in the temples. One example is the jade mask above. The face has a charm that people today would not think of as being from the Aztecs. There is no doubt that the artist wanted this image to be a sign of the scary nature of the god.

Statue of an Eagle Warrior. It's now in the Museum of Anthropology in Mexico City. Photo: Maunus

A four piece life-sized statue of an eagle warrior also shows the Aztec ability to make simple forms that are not like the others. This piece shows how good the Aztecs were at making large sculptures. The image was once painted and covered in feathers. The figure may have been more like the costumed gods as they were in Aztec painting.

Statue of the Jaguar Cuauhxicalli. It's now in the Museum of Anthropology in Mexico City. Photo: Luidger

One of the most amazing Aztec sculptures is a Jaguar. It was made to hold the hearts of people who passed away. The Jaguar shows the earth getting offerings. Jaguar skins were part of the dress of Aztec kings. Therefore the animal came to show royalty. It is thought that this statue showed the links between the new times and the gods of the past.

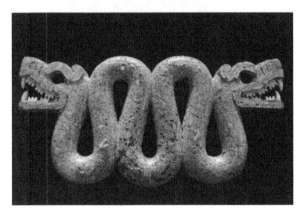

Double-headed Serpent Pectoral. It's in the British Museum in London.

The Aztec craftsmen were good at carving hard stone. From the southern part of the empire, the Aztecs got taxes in the form of jade and obsidian. From these stones they made colorful jewelry for the priests and rulers. The two-headed serpent pendant was made by putting turquoise on a wood base. The red spots on the serpents head are colored shells. This item shows the twin serpents with the feathered serpent god. He is the best known of the Aztec gods today.

Chapter 5: The Spanish Conquest

Hernan Cortes

Cortés, the conqueror of Mexico, set sail to make himself rich with the gold of the new world. With 11 ships, he sailed around the Yucatan Peninsula of modern Mexico and then moved on to Tabasco. There he fought and quickly beat the natives. He demanded 20 young native women be given to him as slaves. One of them, called La Malinche, was fluent in the Mayan and the Aztec languages. She would serve as his translator as he marched over Mexico.

Cortés sailed up the east coast of Mexico and took control over the Spanish outpost at Veracruz. He became separate from the command of the Governor of Cuba. He placed himself under the command of King Charles V of Spain. Having learned of a rich kingdom in the jungle, Cortés burned his ships to make it impossible to go back. Then he set off with 500 men, a few horses and 15 cannons. On the way, Cortés fought and made peace with tribes he met. Among them were the Tlaxcalteca. They gave him 3,000 soldiers. Of course, the Aztecs had many enemies in the area and across much of Mexico. The Spanish were seen as saviors, not enemies.

After getting to the Valley of Mexico, Cortés attacked the large city of Cholula. There he killed many of its 100,000 inhabitants. They also burned it down and destroyed 365 temples. He then marched to the Aztec city of Tenochtitlan. When his men arrived at the lakeshore they were shocked at the sight. Much later one of Cortés' soldiers, Bernal Diaz del Castillo, wrote, "We saw so many cities and villages built both on the water and on dry land, and a straight, level [bridge to Tenochtitlan], we couldn't resist our admiration. It was like the [story] in the book... because of the high towers, pyramids and other buildings, all of masonry, which rose from the water. Some of our soldiers asked if what we saw was not a dream."

Cortes was greeted by men sent by the Aztec king, Montezuma II, and invited to enter his great city of Tenochtitlan. Montezuma may have been afraid of Cortés. Or, he thought Cortés was the Toltec god who would come from the east to destroy the Aztecs.

Letting the Spanish in was a mistake. The Aztec king made another mistake by putting his guests in the palace. Wandering around the fancy guest rooms, the Spanish found a room full of treasure. They began to get ready for a fight.

The Spanish soon found their excuse. When they saw the Aztecs killing their own people, they knew they had to stop it. They took Montezuma prisoner. When the people got upset, the Spanish took him out in front of them to calm them down. In the riot that followed, he was hit by a rock and died.

The riot got worse. Cortés and his men fought their way out of Tenochtitlan and to the mainland. They then cut off the food supply to the city. Finally, they defeated many Aztecs, and took all the treasure they could put their hands on. Then they destroyed what was left of the city.

Cortés went on to then attack and wipe out cities in the Valley of Mexico that had been friends with the Aztecs. To top it all off, the Aztecs caught diseases from the Spanish, and many of them died. In just a few years, the Aztec empire had been completely wiped out.

Made in the USA
Monee, IL
06 November 2022

17255756R00036